W9-CDL-747

this book belongs to:

2022 - ALL RIGHTS RESERVED

Goodbye
tension
Hello
pension

OFFICIALLY
RETIRED
FROM THE
CRAP

LET THE
FUN
BEGINS

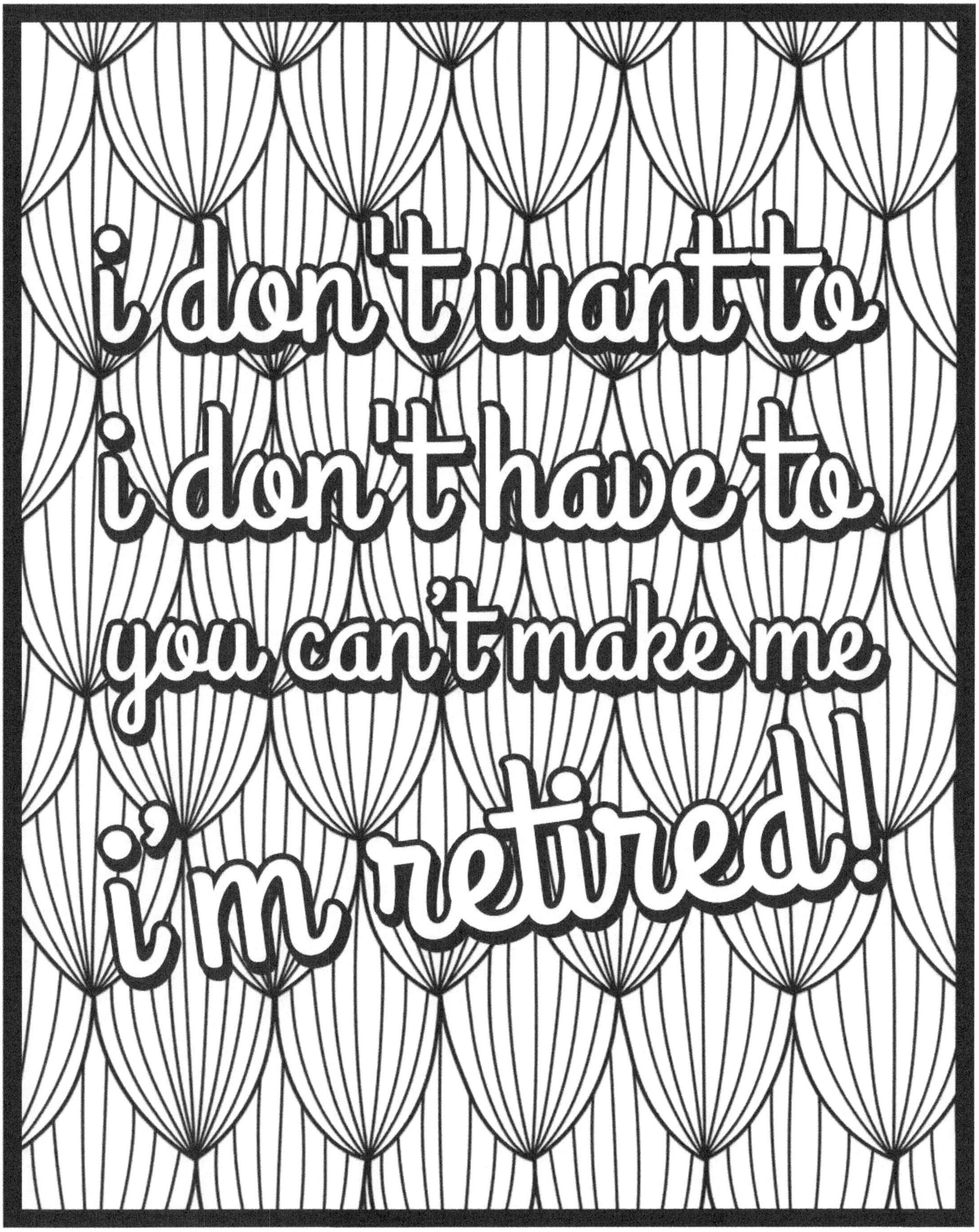
i don't want to
i don't have to
you can't make me
i'm retired!

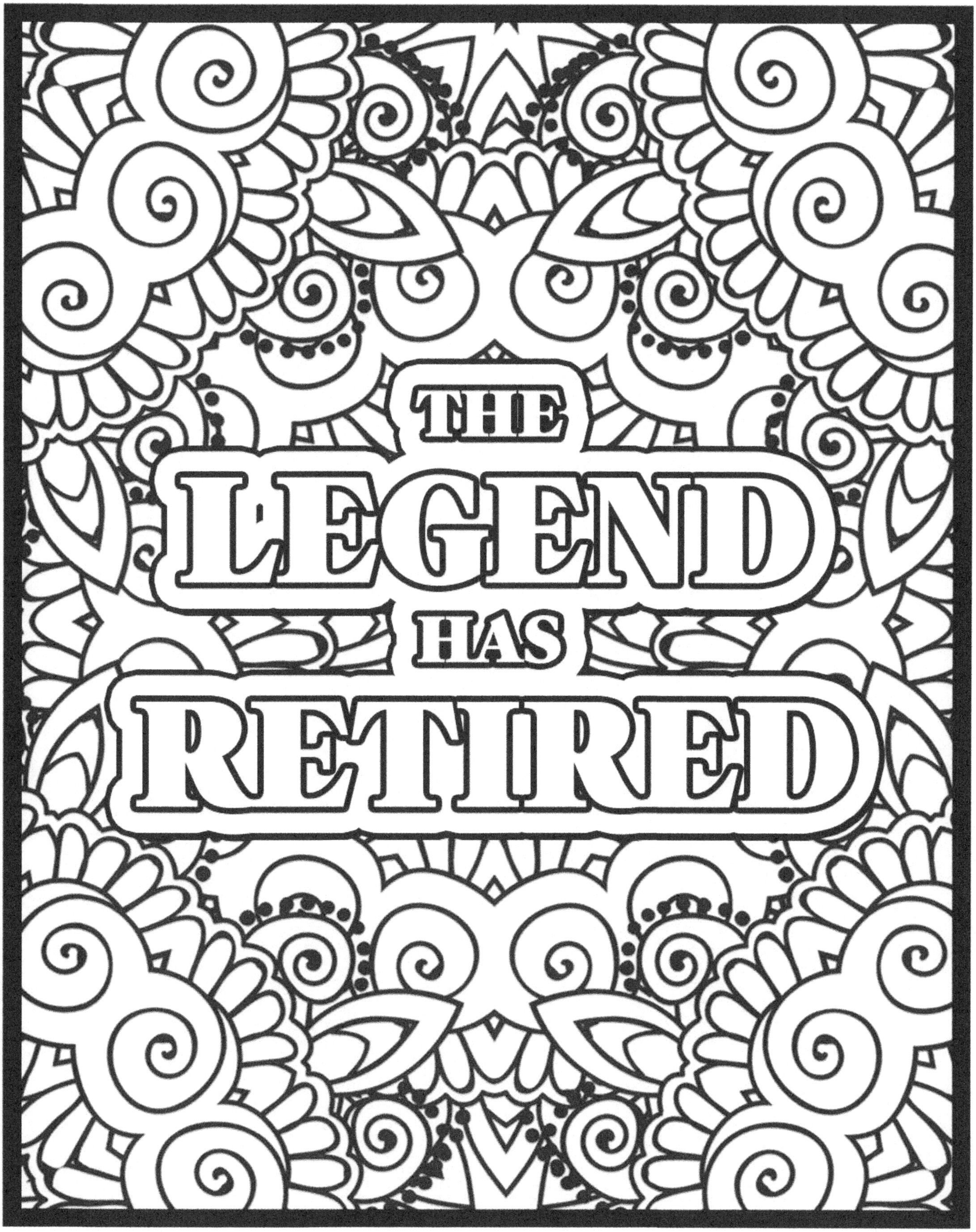
THE
LEGEND
HAS
RETIRED

WHAT DAY IS
TODAY?
WHO CARES.
I'M RETIRED

DON'T
DISTURB
I'M RETIRED

I Love Mondays

You Can't Retire from Being
awesome!

DON'T
ASK ME
TO DO A
DAMN
THING

STFU!
JUST ASSUME
I'M ALWAYS
RIGHT

Every Hour is a Happy Hour

HAPPY
Retirement

WHAT DO YOU
CALL A PERSON
WHO IS HAPPY
ON A MONDAY?
Retired

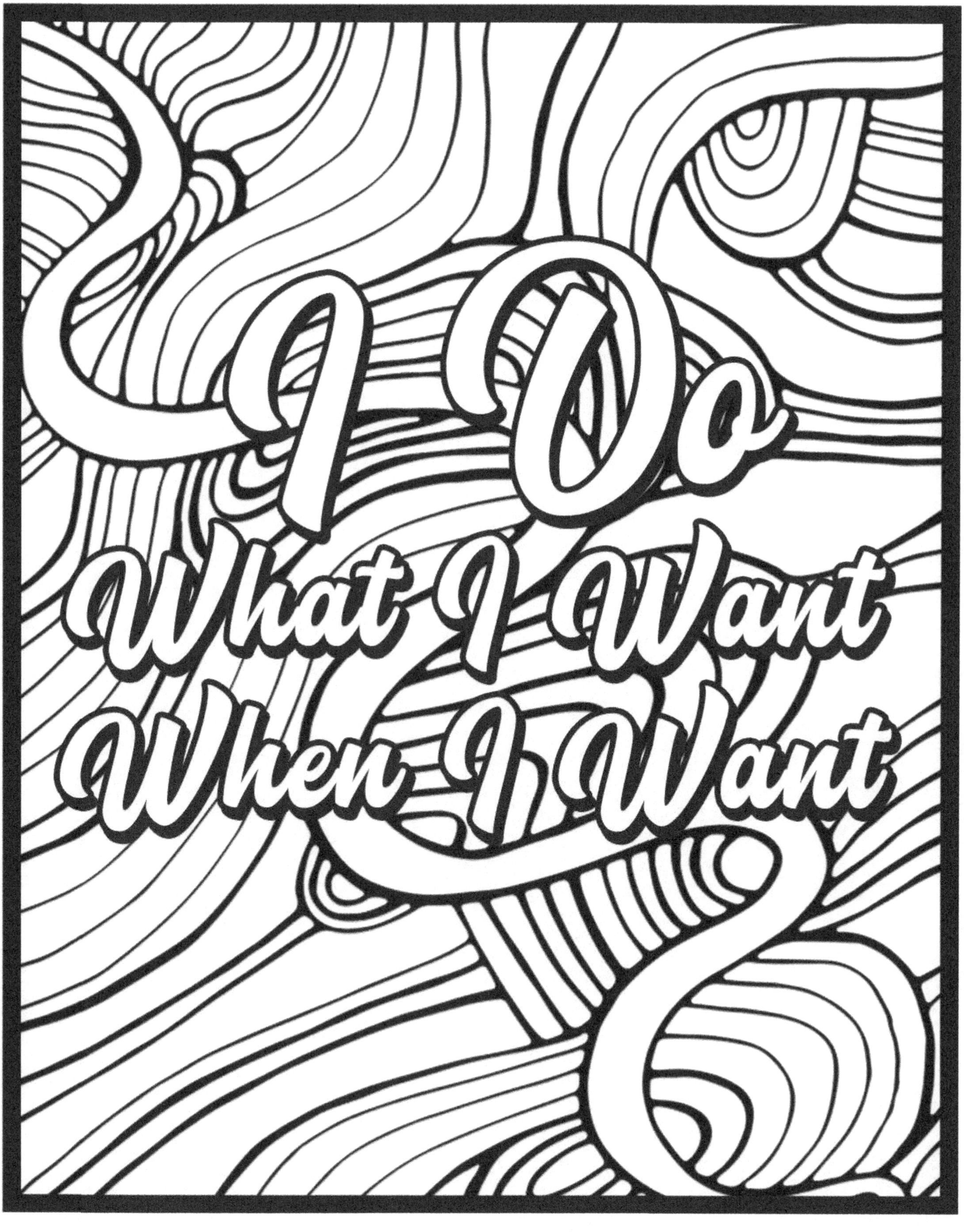
I Do
What I Want
When I Want

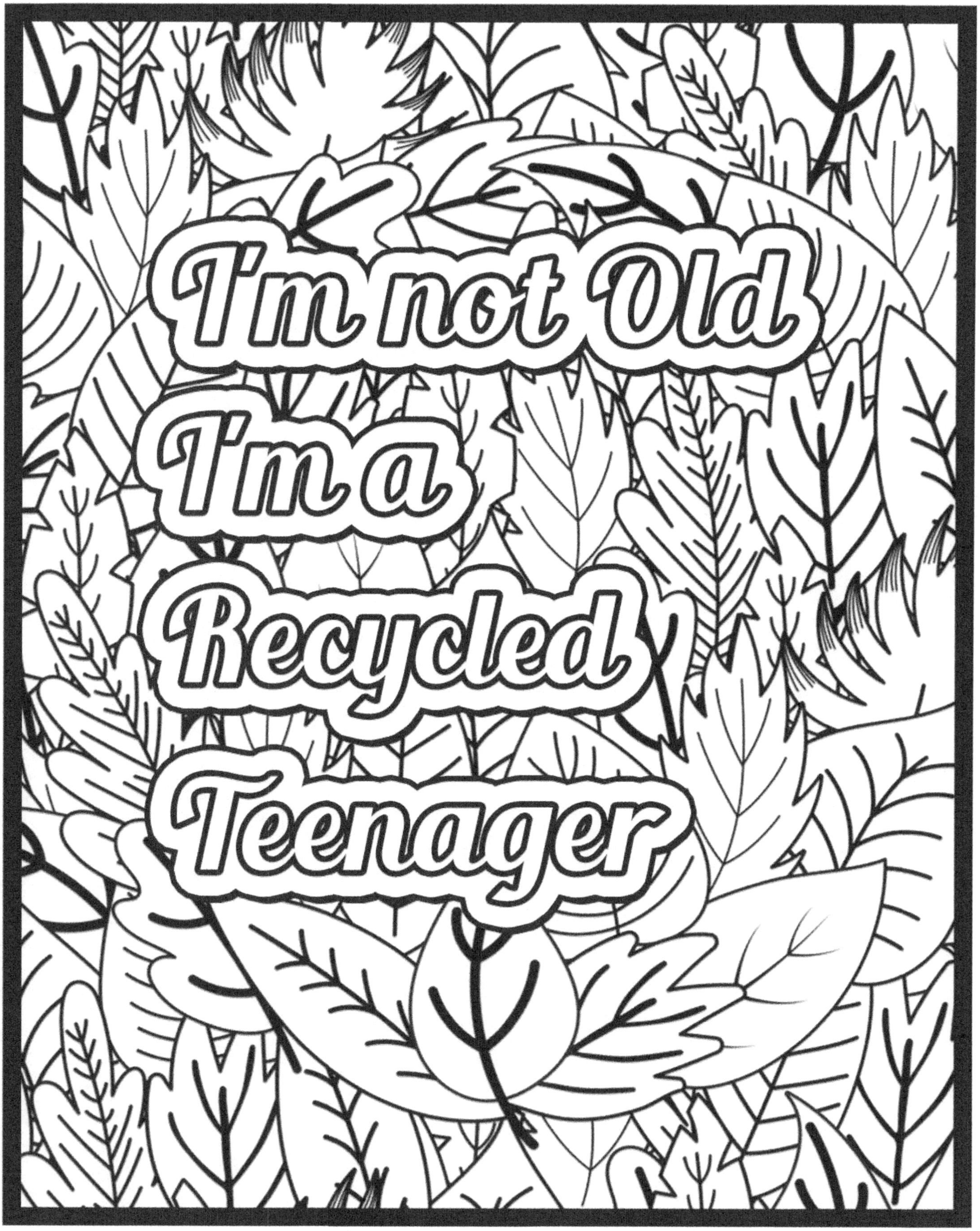
I'm not Old
I'm a
Recycled
Teenager

OLD
LIVES
MATTER

not my
problem
anymore

Free
and
Fabulous

Retired
Under New
Management
See My Wife
For Details

Made in the USA
Monee, IL
10 December 2022

20821691R10024